## TABLE OF CONTENTS

# STRATEGIC IMPLICATIONS OF USING MILITARY TRIBUNALS TO BRING INTERNATIONAL TERRORISTS TO JUSTICE

"The dogmas of the quiet past are inadequate to the stormy present. The occasion is piled high with difficulty, and we must rise with the occasion. As our case is new, so we must think anew, and act anew. We must disenthrall ourselves and then we shall save our country"

—Abraham Lincoln

Globalization and failed states, as well as other changes, will challenge the future security of the United States in the 21st century. On September 11, 2001, the United States was moved from the "dogmas of the quiet past" after fears of a catastrophic terrorist attack against the United States unfortunately came true. The unprecedented nature of the September 11 attacks and the magnitude of damage and loss of life have thrust our nation into the "stormy present." Seen as the only way to deal with the power and influence of the United States, our opponents will continue to challenge us asymmetrically using terrorism as a weapon to wage war.[1]

Our nation responded to the September 11 attacks by developing a military response and building an international coalition to fight a global war on terrorism. In his September 20, 2001 speech before a joint session of Congress, President Bush declared that "whether we bring our enemies to justice or bring justice to our enemies, justice will be done."[2] Furthermore, in his State of the Union Address on January 30, 2002, the President stated that one of the main objectives in the war on terrorism will be to "shut down terrorist camps, disrupt terrorist plans and bring terrorists to justice."[3] The September 11 attacks clearly violated numerous laws that could be prosecuted as criminal acts, just as past terrorists acts have been prosecuted in the United States. However, due to the horrendous circumstances of September 11, many assert that the acts are not just criminal acts, but are "acts of war."

On November 13, 2001, President Bush signed a Military Order that specified instructions for the detention, treatment, and trial of certain non-citizens as part of the global war on terrorism. The order states that effective conduct of military operations and prevention of military attacks make it necessary to detain certain non-citizens and, if necessary, try them "for violations of the laws of war and other applicable laws by military tribunals."[4] This broad Military Order, patterned after similar actions taken by Presidents Abraham Lincoln and Franklin D. Roosevelt, gives the government the power to try, sentence and execute suspected foreign terrorists in secrecy, under special rules that deny them constitutional rights, and allows no chance for appeal. Pursuant to the Military Order, the President alone will decide who will go before a military tribunal. Since one of the end states in this new asymmetric global war on terrorism involves many coalition nations throughout the world, will this be an effective way for the United States and the world to bring justice to terrorists? Just as prior military tactics and equipment had to be modified in order to adapt to this new asymmetric warfare, we may also have to "think anew" about how to use legal tools that are available to bring these terrorists to justice.

Supporters argue that military tribunals are a constitutional necessity to address terrorism of an unprecedented scope. Opponents claim that the tribunals would undermine the rule of law and deprive defendants of the protection provided in the American system of justice. This paper will explore the positive and negative arguments for instituting the use of military tribunals to prosecute suspected terrorists during armed conflicts and how those tribunals may affect future strategic implications. There are those who may disagree with certain conclusions in this paper, particularly those of the legal profession or experts in international law. I am not an expert in the field of law or international law; rather, I am a concerned citizen and soldier who is interested in the most effective way to bring terrorists involved in this new global asymmetric war to justice.

As a point of clarification, the Manual for Courts-Martial, which governs trial by courts-martial, refers to tribunals as "commissions." The term "military commission" will be used throughout this paper and will be synonymous with the term "military tribunal."

## THE HISTORY AND EVOLUTION OF MILITARY COMMISSIONS

Before conducting an analysis of possible strategic implications of using military commissions, I will first provide a brief background on the history of the legal basis for military commissions, historical precedents establishing the use of military commissions, and the law of war.

LEGAL BASIS FOR ESTABLISHING MILITARY COMMISSIONS

The United States adheres to the law of war through incorporation of the customary rules and treaty provisions into regulations of the armed forces. The United States Army Field Manual FM 27-10, *Law of Land Warfare*, may be viewed as an embodiment of the United States Army's interpretation of the law of war on land.[5] Military jurisdiction is recognized from two sources: "that branch of a country's municipal law which recognizes its military establishment" and "that which is derived from international law, including the law of war."[6] The United States military exercises it jurisdiction through the use of courts-martial, military commissions, provost courts, and other military tribunals.[7]

A military commission consists of a panel of military officers convened by military authority to try enemy belligerents on charges of a violation of the law of war.[8] It is distinct from a military courts-martial, which is a panel set up to try only U.S. service members for violations of the Uniformed Code of Military Justice. In contrast to a military commission used for enemy belligerents, U.S. service members charged with a violation of the law of war may be tried either before a courts-martial or in a United States Federal Court.[9]

Jurisdiction over military commissions comes from the Constitution and international law. International law includes the law of war. The Manual for Courts-Martial provides that, subject to any applicable rule of international law or to any regulations prescribed by the President, military commissions shall be guided by the appropriate principles of law and rules of procedures and evidence prescribed for courts-martial. Generally, the power of the President to convene military commissions, along with establishing the procedures used in these commissions, flows from his authority as Commander-in-Chief of the Armed Forces and his responsibility to execute the laws of the nation.[10] The President has the authority to convene any number of military commissions in response to crimes or atrocities during a declared state of war.

HISTORICAL PRECEDENTS

The proposed military commission has its roots in historical and legal precedents that condone treating enemy spies and infiltrators as "unlawful belligerents" and that give the government virtually unlimited wartime power to detain and deport non-citizens suspected of subversive activities. Most of the United States' experience with military commissions relates to occupied territory or conditions of martial law. Although the September 11 terrorist attacks do not fit typical circumstances associated with war crimes, there is some precedent for convening military commissions to try enemy belligerents for conspiring to commit violations of the law of war outside of any recognized war zone.

During the occupation of Mexico in 1847, General Winfield Scott convened "councils of war" to try Mexican citizens accused of violations of the law of war, such as committing guerrilla warfare or enticing American soldiers to desert.[11] Despite the lack of statutory authority, General Scott relied on his own power under the law of war as the occupier of territory to issue the order.[12]

In April 1863, President Lincoln issued Union Army General Order Number 100, which declared that military commissions could prosecute "cases which do not come within the Rules and Articles of War, or the jurisdiction conferred by statute on courts-martial" by using the common law of war.[13]  Military commissions tried more than 2,000 cases during the war and reconstruction period.[14]  However, after the war, the courts limited the jurisdiction to areas occupied by United States forces and governed by martial law, and limited the jurisdiction to genuine violations of the law of war.[15]  Not all military commissions were actually needed and may have been counter productive.  One of the more dubious commissions involved Dr. Samuel Mudd.

> John Wilkes Booth broke his leg while fleeing after shooting President Abraham Lincoln, stopping at Mudd's Maryland farm.  He was in disguise and in great pain. Dr. Mudd set his leg and Booth continued his flight.  When Dr. Mudd heard about the assassination of Lincoln, he notified Union troops that a man with a broken leg had been at this farm.  Mudd was arrested by the military and tried by a military tribunal for conspiracy to murder Lincoln and for traitorously aiding his assassin.[16]

The post World War II response to war crimes included both national and international military commissions.  While the Nuremberg War Crimes Tribunal was the most visible venue in the European theater, the number of national military commissions far exceeded the number of trials conducted in the international commissions.  One such national military commission established the authority to try enemy saboteurs caught within the territory of the United States during the war.  After eight Nazi saboteurs were caught by the Coast Guard in 1942, President Franklin D. Roosevelt issued a proclamation that all such enemy saboteurs would be tried by a military commission.[17]  The eight German saboteurs (one of whom was purportedly a United States citizen) were tried by military commission for entering the United States by submarine, shedding their military uniforms, and conspiring to use explosives on unknown targets.  They were tried as "unlawful combatants," a phrase that originated in this case by the United States but to this day does not appear in the Geneva Conventions.  In the case of *Ex Parte Quirin*, the Supreme Court denied their writs of *habeas corpus*, holding that trial by such a commission did not offend the Constitution and was authorized by statue.[18]  Six of the eight saboteurs were subsequently hanged.

After World War II, the Tokyo Trials, along with the Nuremberg Trials and the Nazis' prosecution, represented an unprecedented effort to punish people accused of war crimes and crimes against humanity.  Prior to Nuremberg, jurisdiction over such offenses was limited to individual countries' military courts.[19]  For the first time, the concepts of collective guilt and conspiracy were used to justify punishment.  The Nuremberg and Tokyo trials were considered revolutionary because they represented the first organized attempt to apply principles of

4

international law.[20]  Since few such laws existed before the trials, prosecutors often were forced to establish new precedents in order to justify convictions.[21]

An eleven nation tribunal was set up in Tokyo after the World War II to prosecute Japanese officials who had overseen that nation's military aggression throughout Asia.  Among the atrocities blamed on those officials was the so called Rape of Nanking, when Japanese soldiers slaughtered hundreds of thousands of Chinese civilians in Nanking, China in 1937. Seven of the twenty-eight defendants in the Tokyo war crimes trials were sentenced to death; the others received prison sentences.

After World War II, the Nuremberg and Tokyo War Crimes tribunals brought nations to again discuss a permanent war crimes tribunal and to set in motion the creation of a permanent international criminal court.[22]  This was the case, even though the Nuremberg and Tokyo war crimes tribunals differed in many ways from a permanent, standing international criminal court. Prior to the creation of the United Nations, military tribunals were ad hoc in composition and were "victors courts."[23]  The Nuremberg Trials established a legacy for future war crimes tribunals in the area of individual responsibility for war crimes in the conduct of warfare.[24]

LAW OF WAR

Can the attacks of September 11, 2001, be considered "acts of war" under international law and if so, how will those responsible be treated under the law of war?  The law of war has deep historical roots from two sources: treaties and custom.[25]  The idea that some methods of warfare are illegal is comparatively modern.

> As any reader of the Old Testament, Thucydides, Caesar, or Livy knows, ancient history is full of appalling chronicles of rapine, pillage and massacre – some of it not merely permitted, but practically mandatory under contemporary notions of morality.  When Marcus Crassus put a definitive end to Spartacus' revolt by crucifying six thousand captive slaves along the road from Capua to Rome, it would not have occurred to Cicero or anyone else to call him a criminal; the Senate decreed him a triumph.[26]

The first attempt to codify the law of war is generally accepted to be the first Geneva Convention of 1864.[27]  The process continued with the Hague Conventions of 1899 and 1907, and took the form we recognize today when the Geneva Convention was revised and expanded into the four Geneva Conventions of 1949.  Army Field Manual 27-10, *The Law of Land Warfare*, codifies the United States Army's interpretation of the law of war, incorporating reference to the relevant conventions and rules of the customary law of war, as well as relevant statutes.[28]

The law of war may be applied only to acts that are part of an "armed conflict." A terrorist act is not considered to be an act of war unless it is part of a broader campaign of violence directed against the state. Where terrorist acts amount to no more than situations of internal disturbances and tensions such as riots and isolated and sporadic acts of violence, the Hague and Geneva Conventions do not apply.[29]

There are two recognized types of armed conflicts – international and internal. Because the terrorist organization behind the September 11 attacks is not a state under international law and its members are not uniformed soldiers of any recognized army, there are conceptual difficulties in fitting their activities into the rubric of the international law of war.[30]

The present conflict does not fit squarely within the definition of internal or international armed conflicts. The attacks on New York, Pennsylvania, and the Pentagon do not appear to have been part of an effort to take control of territory or install a new government, nor is it certain that they were carried out under the direction of another state. However, the sophisticated planning and execution believed necessary to have accomplished the attacks suggest that they were carried out by organized members of a quasi-military force.[31] Assuming the existence of an armed conflict, it is beyond question that the September 11 attacks were part of it. Preparation for the attacks would also be covered, notwithstanding the fact that the hostilities had not yet technically begun.[32] A new paradigm may be necessary to incorporate terrorism into the legal structure of warfare.

## WAR, MILITARY COMMISSIONS, AND TERRORISM

In order to prosecute war crimes by military commissions for "acts of war," a state of war has to exist. In the context of the war on terrorism, the term *war* is "a metaphor to signify struggle, commitment, and endurance," according to Michael Walzer, author of the classic book *Just and Unjust Wars*.[33] Could this still be a metaphorical war if the Commander-in-Chief, in his 20 September 2001 address before a joint session of Congress, declared war on global terrorism along with the declaration being quickly supported by a joint Congressional resolution supporting the use of force? If those responsible for the attacks of September 11, 2001, are to be treated under the law of war, what constitutes a war?

There is no court case or treaty that conclusively answers the question or defines war.[34] Only Congress can declare war, which it has not done. Can a state of war exist without a congressional declaration? On the basis of history alone, the answer is yes.[35] The United States, which has employed military force more than 220 times in its history, has declared war only five times, most recently more than a half a century ago.[36] Even if military commissions

6

can be used in a war that exists in absence of a congressional declaration, can war be made on an individual or non-state group such as terrorists?  The opposite is also important: can individuals or non-state actors declare war?

The September 11 attacks that destroyed the World Trade Center and damaged the Pentagon have been universally condemned as barbarous acts. They are also fundamental breaches of international humanitarian law, which governs the rules of armed conflict. Yet the rapid resort by political leaders to use the terminology of war has caused both the public and some other governments to question whether the attacks are to be viewed first and foremost as acts of war under international law, as terrorist acts, or criminal acts.[37]

In 1801, President Thomas Jefferson made undeclared war on the Barbary pirates. Although in this one instance the war was declared on individuals, the United States traditionally has viewed individuals and terrorists as common law criminals.[38]  Terrorism is not mentioned in Army Field Manual 27-10, *The Law of Land Warfare* and the 1949 Geneva Conventions. However, on September 11, 2001, the United States and the world declared that terrorism graduated from a criminal act to a military attack.  Even the United Nations, in rare support of the use of force, supports the war and has voted to require United Nations members to act against terrorism.[39]  Furthermore, reflecting evolving international law, there has been virtually no criticism of the war on terrorism.[40]  Taking into consideration that the United States and the world agree that a war exists against global terrorists, military commissions are authorized to prosecute war crimes or "acts of war."  Since the attack of September 11, 2001, terrorism graduated from criminality to a clear cut military attack.  Still, there is an issue concerning whether captured terrorists are prisoners of war or "unlawful combatants," both of which would make them eligible to be prosecuted by military commissions.

To shed some light on whether or not al Qaeda and Taliban "detainees" qualify for POW status, most legal experts cite *Article 4 of the 1949 Geneva Convention*, which defines prisoners of war as "Members of the armed forces of a Party to the conflict as well as members of militias or volunteer corps forming part of such armed forces."[41]  According to the Convention, members of a regular army are automatically entitled to prisoner of war status, whereas members of militias or volunteer corps must meet the following four criteria:

- Have a chain of command
- Wear a uniform or some sort fixed or distinctive sign
- Carry their arms openly
- Conduct their operations in accordance with the laws and customs of war

Most legal experts believe that the Taliban fall under the first category, being the regular army of Afghanistan, and are therefore entitled to prisoner of war status. Current government policies claim that the Taliban fall under the category of irregular forces, and therefore are subject to meeting the four criteria.

But even according to the criteria specified for irregular forces, most legal experts believe the Taliban detainees, and possibly al Qaeda as well, would be entitled to prisoner of war status. They cite *Article 5 of the 1949 Geneva Convention*, which says that if there is any doubt as to whether or not the detainees meet the conditions, then they should be granted prisoner of war status until a "competent tribunal" determines otherwise.[42] Most legal experts believe that the United States has little to gain by denying the detainees prisoner of war status.[43] The distinctions matter. International humanitarian law, which in its present form reflects the lessons of the Holocaust and World War II and is codified in the form of the Geneva Conventions and other universally accepted treaties, sets out the binding criteria that determine what is legal, illegal, and criminal in armed conflict.[44] It also defines crimes against humanity and genocide, abominations that can occur in war or in peacetime.

Terrorism, murder, and hijacking are domestic crimes within the jurisdiction of the United States district courts and are federal offenses. Murder, hijacking, and genocide, when committed by combatants, also are violations of the law of armed conflict that can be tried using military commissions under Article 18 of the Uniform Code of Military Justice (UCMJ), which is also federal law.[45] Article 21 of the UCMJ recognizes the military commissions' jurisdiction to try only "offenders or offenses that by statute or by the law of war may be tried by military commissions."[46] Therefore, references to "offenses" and "crimes" in President Bush's November 13, 2001 Military Order must be understood to refer to "offenses against the law of war" and "war crimes," or to those offenses mentioned expressly by statute as able to be prosecuted by military commissions.[47] Since the United States and the world agree that a war exists against global terrorists, captured terrorists are not domestic common law criminals. They should be identified as prisoners of war, and should be treated and prosecuted for war crimes under the internationally accepted provisions of the Geneva Conventions.

## ARGUMENTS IN FAVOR OF INSTITUTING MILITARY COMMISSIONS TO PROSECUTE SUSPECTED TERRORISTS DURING ARMED CONFLICTS

> "In 1780, General George Washington, commanding an army fighting against tyranny and injustice, ordered the execution of Major John Andre, an accused British spy, after a hasty trial in a special military commission."
>
> —Stuart Taylor Jr.

Like presidents before him, President Bush has invoked his authority as Commander-in-Chief, under Article 2 of the United States Constitution, to establish military commissions to try enemy belligerents who commit war crimes. The government argues that in appropriate circumstances, these commissions provide important advantages over civilian trials. The Supreme Court has consistently upheld the use of military commissions. Strangely enough, even though many people in the United States and abroad may find fault with the legal profession, they have an abiding faith in the American courts of justice. They seem to feel that if a wrong is threatened or committed, redress can be secured, even in times of war. But never before have we anticipated action against terrorists who may have committed murderous actions against targets in the United States and on foreign soil. Many argue that the ability of the criminal justice system to deal with this threat on its own has never been more apparent.[48]

Nevertheless, we have so far treated terrorists as ordinary criminals, charging them with common law crimes and given them all the protections of our criminal justice system. The 1993 World Trade Center attack, for example, led to indictments that were tried before a judge in the Southern District of New York.

In certain circumstances, military commissions provide important advantages over civilian trials. Many contend that the time has come to treat terrorists as members of organized enemy forces who act with complete disregard for the laws of war. Proponents claim that we should abandon our previous strategy of pursuing common criminal prosecutions alone and adopt a wartime approach under international law.[49] As with all things, the law of war has evolved past traditional limitations; combatants no longer wear uniforms or are members of a nation's armed forces to be liable for war crimes.[50] Using military commissions would spare American jurors, judges, and courts the risks associated with terrorist trials.[51] While jurors are supposed to be anonymous, they could easily end up living in fear. Witnesses in such cases are, if necessary, placed in the federal witness protection program. Proponents for military commissions contend they are necessary to shield the government from the necessity of revealing classified information. According to George Terwilliger, former Deputy Attorney General, "We have circumstances here where we cannot protect the intelligence sources and methods that we need to protect in order to preempt further acts without protecting the evidentiary basis that is used in these trials."[52] Advocates for military commissions point out that the time has come to use these commissions because they have numerous advantages over civilian courts.

COMPARING A MILITARY COMMISSION TO A COURTS-MARTIAL OR CIVILIAN COURT

- A federal trial is generally open to the public, while a military commission may be closed. Advocates of the military commission process say such a setting denies a public forum to the accused.

- Military commissions are not secret. The President's Military Order authorizes the Secretary of Defense to close proceedings to protect classified information. It does not require that any trial, or even portions of a trial, be conducted in secret. Trials are normally open, consistent with the needs of national security.

- A military commission may be held in a different country, in a territory such as Guam or on a U.S. naval ship.

- Greater security can be imposed over what information is disclosed in a military commission as compared with a federal prosecution.

- Like a courts-martial, a military commission will be composed of military members, ostensibly only officer members and usually no fewer than five, the minimum number that can sit for a general courts-martial.

- Unlike a federal prosecution, a person tried by a military commission does not have the right to a jury trial.

- A military commission's findings of guilt or imposition of the death penalty does not have to be unanimous. In the case of a five-member panel, four of the members could vote guilty and impose the death penalty.

- The death penalty may be imposed immediately.

- Unlike due process provision in the United States judicial system, a person tried by a military commission will have no right to appeal a conviction.

Advocates contend that military commissions do not undermine the constitutional values of civil liberties or separation of powers; they protect them by ensuring that the United States may wage war against external enemies and defeat them. To defend the nation, the President has rightly sought to employ every lawful means at his disposal; military commissions are one such means, and their judicious use will help keep Americans safe and free.[53]

Although numerous lawyers strongly advocate using military commissions, many lawyers state the proposed commissions are significantly different from courts-maritals. According to John S. Cooke, a retired army judge who is the chairman of the American Bar Association's Committee on Armed Forces Law, "these proposed military commissions are a totally different animal."[54] Standard military courts closely resemble civilian courts in many ways; many of the fundamental protections afforded by military courts were ignored in the President's November 13, 2001 Military Order authorizing military commissions.[55]

## ARGUMENTS AGAINST INSTITUTING MILITARY COMMISSIONS TO PROSECUTE SUSPECTED TERRORISTS DURING ARMED CONFLICTS

"We stand for a great deal in this country....When we are talking about setting aside our criminal justice system for something like these proposed military commissions, we end up looking to the people we have asked to be our allies more and more like some of the things that we are fighting against

—Senator Patrick Leahy, ranking member, Senate Judiciary Committee

The words of Justice Robert Jackson, uttered at the opening of the Nuremberg trials fifty-five years ago, seems to reflect the concern stated above by Senator Leahy and numerous others when he said, "stay the hand of vengeance and voluntarily submit their captive enemies to the judgment of law is one of the most significant tributes that Power has ever paid to reason. We must never forget that the record on which we judge these defendants is the record on which history will judge us tomorrow."[56] Although many favor using military commissions to bring terrorists to justice, there seem to be many more that are vehemently against using military commissions. In a letter that originated at Yale Law School, more than 300 law professors from around the country assert that such military commissions are "legally deficient, unnecessary and unwise."[57] These legal scholars do not favor military commissions because they state the commissions place little emphasis on procedural safeguards, exclusionary rules, and the right to a vigorous defense in favor of a more streamlined system with fewer safeguards and fewer acquittals.

Under President Bush's November 13, 2001 Military Order, he has directed the Secretary of Defense to set all the rules for the military commissions, including how many members will be on the panel, what qualifications they must meet, what standard of proof will be needed to convict, and what type of evidence can be considered, along with no judicial review.[58] Only the President or Secretary of Defense will have the authority to overturn a decision. The one rule that is very specific is that the accused can be convicted and sentenced to life in prison or death if two-thirds of the panel agrees.[59] The problem with this Military Order is that it does not clearly limit its application to those accused of war crimes, leaving open the possibility that the government wrongly sought to extend military jurisdiction beyond its settled limits. The order also left unstated whether a presumption of innocence would apply, what rights defendants would have to know the charges and evidence against them, and to see their attorneys.[60] Major

11

strategic implications and issues of contention concerning these proposed military commissions center around secrecy, lack of judicial review, and only two-thirds vote to impose the death penalty.

One of the most basic internationally recognized tenets of justice requires that criminal proceedings be open to the public and that evidence against the accused be revealed to the defendant. The International Military Tribunal at Nuremberg tried and convicted Nazi leaders in public proceedings in which the defendants were able to hear the evidence against them in a language they could understand.[61] They were entitled to the assistance of counsel and had the right to cross-examine witnesses called by the prosecution.[62] Critics of the current plan state that military commissions could be closed on order of the Secretary of Defense, defendants could be convicted based on secret evidence, and there are no provisions for assistance of counsel or the right of cross-examination.

The most negative strategic implication we could send to our allies and the rest of the world would be to implement totally secret commissions, which the government says it wants to avoid but refuses to rule out. Such secret commissions would make it next to impossible for the United States to protest unfair trials abroad. When Lori Berenson, a young woman from New York, was arrested in Peru six years ago, brought before a secret military commission on charges of aiding terrorists and sentenced to life imprisonment without parole, the United States howled in outrage.[63] Whatever she may have done, we argued, she didn't get a fair trial. Similarly, the President's Military Order decreeing the use of closed-door military commissions for foreign terrorism suspects is widely seen in Europe as draconian.[64] Furthermore, these transatlantic differences highlight a long-existing values gap that could of all things complicate the United States efforts to form a unified global law enforcement front in efforts against terrorism.[65] The United States has long preached the same theme: secret military commissions with no judicial review, almost by definition, do not meet minimum standards of justice.[66]

While Congress has enacted procedures applicable to courts-martial that ensure basic due process rights, no such statutory procedures exist to define due process rights for defendants before military commissions. President Bush's Military Order has chosen to cut out judicial review; there will be no appeals to any United States court or to any international commission. What will we say to those who note the contrast between the lack of fundamental fairness and our long history of vocal concerns about the lack of a fair justice system in other countries? As David Scheffer, a senior fellow at the United States Institute of Peace stated, "The world and our allies are watching, we have to be careful that we do to not emerge from this

12

process with a hypocritical administration of justice."[67]  The best way we assure fairness in our system is through accountability, which means some process by which defendants can make appeals in federal court.  If military commissions are used, this fundamental right, agreed upon by our nation and our allies, must be incorporated in rules concerning these commissions.

Another potential strategic implication and problem for the United States specified in the military order creating these military commissions deals with not only allowing the death penalty, but also the provision requiring less than unanimous (two-thirds) vote for execution.  European governments in particular simply will not extradite terrorists to any jurisdiction where the death penalty would be available upon conviction.[68]  France, Britain, Germany, Italy, Belgium and Spain are holding people allegedly linked to the al Qaeda terrorist network and are suspected of involvement in other terrorists plots against European and American targets.[69]  The fifteen European Union countries have all abolished the death penalty and generally refuse extradition to the United States unless the death penalty is waived by federal courts.  Implementation of military commissions will greatly hamper not only extradition efforts, but may fracture long standing international law enforcement and legal agreements, further raising worldwide uncertainties.

WORLD-WIDE CONCERNS

In an address to the National Defense University on February 21, 2002, Admiral Dennis C. Blair, Commander-in-Chief of United States Pacific Command, stated that "the United States must seek an unprecedented degree of international cooperation to win the war on terrorism and probe lineages in Asia and around the world between the al Qaeda network and other organized criminals.  Just about everything we do deals with an ally or a partner of some kind"[70] If the United States must depend on allies and other nations to help prosecute the global war on terrorism, provisions governing the rules of military commissions must take international concerns into account.  The European Human Rights Convention, a post World War II treaty that 34 governments have committed to honor, uses language similar to the U.S. Bill of Rights which guarantees public trials, the right to a jury, the right to confront witnesses and the right to an attorney, along with prohibiting the death penalty.[71]  The use of secret military commissions appears to be in direct contradiction to this treaty.

European nations contend that these requirements would not be met if the United States implements the proposed military commissions for trying foreigners accused of terrorism.  Echoing this concern from one of the United States staunchest allies, Christopher Meyer, the British ambassador to the United States, said that his country would be expected to resist extraditing prisoners to the U.S. if they would be subject to secret military commissions and the death penalty.[72]

Criticism over provisions in President Bush's Military Order establishing military commissions has also come from the United Nations. The United Nations Human Rights Commissioner, Mary Robinson, stated that "military commissions must not skirt democratic guarantees and those safeguards, including the right to a fair trial and must be upheld even in our present crises situation. The September 11 terrorist attacks were crimes against humanity meriting special measures but the plan for secret trials is overly broad, vaguely worded and threatens fundamental rights."[73]

Advocates against the November 13, 2001 Military Order signed by President Bush instituting military commissions say it will undermine fundamental and moral democratic values of the United States. European countries have held firm against the proposed military commissions based upon their own laws and the European Convention on Human Rights. If the United States conducts military commissions under the provisions of the November 13 Military Order, it risks losing international support and losing the moral high ground, along with the right to stand up for and condemn other countries for human rights abuses.

## CONCLUSION

> "He that would make his own liberty secure must guard even his enemy from oppression; for if he violates this duty he establishes a precedent that will reach himself."

—Thomas Paine

One of the goals stated in the United States National Security Strategy is to promote democracy, human rights, and respect for the rule of law.[74] The National Security Strategy goes on to state that our core values – political and economic freedom, respect for human rights, and the rule of law – support the belief that individuals should control their own destinies, guiding the conduct of our government at home as well as in its dealings with others outside our borders.[75] What matters in this global war on terrorism is not just how the United States may implement military commissions, but also the impression it leaves throughout the world. It is vital that we are seen as acting in accord with human rights principles along with protecting and preserving American values. One of these values is justice. We have an entire system designed to achieve that.

Military commissions have been used throughout history and have generally been regarded as effective. The problem is there are no "standing rules" that govern military commissions; there have been different rules for commissions throughout history. The Uniformed Code of Military Justice requires a public trial, proof beyond a reasonable doubt, the right to choose a trial by jury, the right to choose counsel, unanimity in death sentencing and the right to appellate review. These rules embody due process, along with our nation's core values and should be applied to any consideration for using military commissions.

Federal courts and military courts-martial both are subject to and employ the Classified Information Procedure Act (CIPA), enacted by Congress with the support of the executive branch.[76] Under the CIPA, whose purpose is to protect classified sources and methods from public disclosure, military commissions, along with federal courts, can close proceedings to protect sensitive information on a case by case basis. Our government has decades of experience and success in using the CIPA in civilian courts to prosecute organized crime and most recently, the prosecution and conviction of terrorists implicated in the 1993 World Trade Center bombing. The procedures using the CIPA have successfully balanced the need to protect classified or sensitive information with the requirements of due process for the accused. Once the CIPA is adopted for proposed military commissions, there should be few objections from Americans or those abroad for holding selected closed military commissions for the purpose of protecting intelligence sources or classified material in support of national security.

Resorting to military commissions as they are currently proposed may prove to be a "mighty swift sword" in our national quest for revenge, but strategic implications will ultimately bring the United States more pain than satisfaction. We are trying to gain the confidence and the support of our allies in the global war on terrorism, along with people in Muslim countries around the world. No nation that refuses to abide by the standards it uses to judge others can plant its feet firmly on the moral high ground. Any country that thinks and behaves otherwise deceives itself.

## RECOMMENDATIONS

> "The moral elements are among the most important in war – they constitute the spirit that permeates war as a whole, and at an early stage they establish a close affinity with the will that moves and lead the whole mass of force, practically merging with it, since the will is itself a moral quantity."

> —Carl von Clausewitz

To win the global war on terrorism the United States must not only physically defeat terrorists world-wide, but must also win the struggle of hearts and minds. The United States can not afford to be seen as hypocritical; trials conducted in secret with no right of appeal will

15

taint world-wide judgment and adversely affect the U.S. position as the world leader for the promotion of human rights. It is not enough for the United States to only be against global terrorism, it must continue to stand for and lead the world in two important aspects – justice and human rights. In order to maintain the moral high ground, the United States must develop a system, possibly with other nations, of specialized courts to handle the judicial aspects of the international terrorist threat. The question is should these new courts evolve out of the military or the civilian systems? I think the answer is that both systems may have a role.

Military commissions are not unfair simply because they are military commissions; one must look at the procedures. The rules and regulations governing the commission determine whether or not they are fair, and whether or not the United States should be concerned. The use of military commissions can be a very effective way to bring terrorists to justice only if the November 13, 2001 Military Order is modified to include basic due process safeguards. These safeguards include the presumption of innocence, proof beyond a reasonable doubt, public proceedings (with narrow exceptions to avert real security breaches), a unanimous verdict to impose a death sentence, a defendant's right to choose his or her own counsel and a right of appeal to the highest military court. As stated earlier in this paper, these protections are already required by the Uniform Code of Military Justice so therefore it should be rather easy to implement. Judges may also include not only military officers but also retired federal judges whose stature and independence is beyond question.

Currently, subject to statutory provisions, the President may establish any procedure and rule of evidence he deems appropriate for a military commission. The problem with this procedure is that different rules and conditions can be established for any number of different military commissions at any time. A possible solution is for Congress to pass legislation that dictates the rules and procedures for conducting future military commissions. Once these rules are established and accepted by not only the United States but also our partners in the international war on terrorism, these standard rules, similar to those stated above under the Uniform Code of Military Justice, will remove world-wide questions of due process rights and further international cooperation to bring terrorists to justice. Although this option would weaken some of the power in the executive branch, it would be a positive step towards removing doubt concerning the rules and procedures for all future military commissions.

Another option to bring justice is the use of United States Federal Courts. Our government has decades of experience and success in using civilian courts to combat organized crime and it has successfully applied that experience to fighting terrorism, most recently by obtaining convictions in the 1993 World Trade Center bombing. Many legal scholars agree that the United States must not be intimidated by the prospect of terrorist trials in U.S. federal court, especially if classified information can be safeguarded.

We need a multifaceted approach to a cancerous problem. Many provisions in the Geneva Conventions do not apply neatly. We need to revise old procedures, used for a different type of warfare and enemy, to a new system dealing with rogue organizations and loosely affiliated non-nation state actors. Another possible solution to the negative strategic implications of implementing military commissions to bring terrorists to justice would be to insist on a hybrid "third way" of international justice, quasi-military courts or an International Crimes Commission that could offer swift justice without diminishing our standards of fairness. Such a court was proposed in the wake of Nuremberg, but interest in the idea had waned by the late 1940s as a result of the Cold War. A new global court, with participants from many nations, would have a broad mandate to prosecute all terrorist related war crimes and human rights violations. To achieve that, as Abraham Lincoln said in another context, "we must think anew and act anew."

If we fail in this regard by instituting a system of justice, whether it is military commissions or an international court that is in accordance with our principles of justice and human rights, we will adversely affect our standing in the world and suffer negative future strategic implications. We need to show the world that we stand by the fundamental principles that this conflict is all about. To forsake justice now is to betray the cause we are fighting for. Verdicts and sentences must have creditability worldwide if the United States national policy is to be a beacon of democracy and human rights to the rest of the world.

WORD COUNT = 7326

# ENDNOTES

[1] William J. Clinton, <u>Presidential Decision Directive 62</u> (Washington, D.C.: The White House, May 1998).

[2] Josh Tyrangiel, "And Justice For...," <u>Time</u>, 26 Nov 2001, 66-67.

[3] Bob Deans, "STATE OF THE UNION ADDRESS: Our War Against Terror Is Only Beginning," <u>The Atlanta Journal – Constitution</u>, 30 Jan 2002, A1.

[4] George W. Bush, <u>Military Order – Detention, Treatment, and Trial of Certain Non-Citizens on the War Against Terrorism</u> (Washington, D.C.: The White House, 13 November 2001).

[5] Department of the Army, <u>Law of Land Warfare</u>, Field Manual 27-10 (Washington: U.S. Department of the Army, July 1956), Chap. 1.

[6] Ibid.

[7] Ibid.

[8] Spencer J. Crona and Niel A. Richardson, "Justice for War Criminals of Invisible Armies: A New Legal and Military Approach to Terrorism," <u>Oklahoma City University Law Review</u>, 1996, 368.

[9] <u>The War Crimes Act of 1996</u>, <u>U.S. Code</u>, 18 U.S.C. 2441 (1996).

[10] United States Constitution, Article II.

[11] Newton, 15.

[12] Ibid.

[13] Ibid., 19.

[14] Ibid.

[15] Ibid., 18.

[16] Phillip A Gagner, "The Bush Administration's Claim That Even Citizens Can Be Brought Before Military Tribunals, And Why It Should Never Be Put Into Practice," 26 December 2001; available from <http://writ.findlaw.com/commentary/20011226 gagner.html>; Internet; accessed 18 February 2002.

[17] Proclamation Number 2561, 2 July 1942, 7 <u>Federal Register</u> 5101, 1964.

[18] Supreme Court Case, <u>Ex Parte Quirin</u>, 317 U.S. 1, 45 (1942).

[19] "War-Crimes Tribunals," 30 November 2001, available from <http://www.2facts.com/IOCF>; Internet; accessed 18 February 2002.

[20] Ibid.

[21] Ibid.

[22] Ellen Grigorian, Congressional Research Service, CRS Report for Congress: The International Criminal Court Treaty: Description, Policy Issues, and Congressional Concerns (Washington, D.C.: Congressional Research Service, Library of Congress, 6 January 1999), 5.

[23] Brigid O'Hara-Forster and Lauren Comiteau, "Justice Goes Global," Time Canada, 27 July 1998, 32.

[24] Mark A. Bland, "An Analysis of the United Nations International Tribunal to Adjudicate War Crimes Committed in Three Former Yugoslavia: Parallels, Problems, Prospects," Global Legal Studies Journal 2, (Spring 1999), 5.

[25] Joseph W. Bishop, Jr., Justice Under Fire, A Study of Military Law (New York: Charterhouse, 1974), 263.

[26] Ibid.

[27] Bartram S. Brown, "Nationality and Internationality in International Humanitarian Law," Stan J. International Law, 1998, 347.

[28] Army Field Manual 27-10, Chap. 1.

[29] Michael P. Scharf, "Defining Terrorism as the Peace Time Equivalent of War Crimes: A Case of Too Much Convergence Between International Humanitarian Law and International Criminal Law," ILSAJ. Intl Law, 2001, 391.

[30] Ruth Wedgewood, "Responding to Terrorism: The Strikes Against bin Laden," Yale J. Intl Law, 1999, 559.

[31] Katherine M. Skiba, "Quick Action Against Bin Laden Called Difficult," Milwaukee Journal Sentinel, 26 September 2001, A6.

[32] Michael A. Newton, "Continuum Crimes: Military Jurisdiction over Foreign Nationals Who Commit International Crimes," Military Law Review, 1996, 20.

[33] Michael Walzer, "First, Define the Battlefield," New York Times, 21 September 2001, sec A, p.35.

[34] Gary D. Solis, "Are We Really at War?" Proceedings, (United States Naval Institute, December 2001), 34.

[35] Ibid.

[36] John N. Moore, National Security Law, (Durham: Durham Carolina Academic Press, 1990),823-824.

[37] "Crimes of War Project," The National Institute of Military Justice, 30 February 2002, available from <http://www.nimj.com/Home.asp>; Internet; accessed 12 March 2002.

[38] Solis, 34.

[39] United Nations Resolution 1373, 28 September 2001.

[40] Solis, 34.

[41] "Crimes of War Project," The National Institute of Military Justice, 30 February 2002, available from <http://www.nimj.com/Home.asp>; Internet; accessed 12 March 2002.

[42] Ibid.

[43] Ibid.

[44] Ibid.

[45] Solis, 34.

[46] Newton, 21.

[47] "Crimes of War Project," The National Institute of Military Justice, 30 February 2002, available from <http://www.nimj.com/Home.asp>; Internet; accessed 12 March 2002.

[48] Michael C. Farkas, "If It's War, Treat It That Way," Proceedings, (United States Naval Institute, December 2001), 34.

[49] Ibid.

[50] Ibid.

[51] Alberto R. Gonzales, "Martial Justice, Full and Fair," New York Times, 30 November 2001,

[52] Stephen Kaufman, "Establishment of Military Tribunals Is Debated in the U.S.," U.S. Department of State, International Information Programs, 28 November 2001, available from <http://usinfo.state.gov/topical/rights/law.htm>; Internet; accessed 22 December 2001.

[53] Gonzales, 10.

[54] William Glaberson, "Tribunal Comparison Taints Courts-Martial, Military Lawyers Say," 2 December 2001, available from <http://partners.nytimes.com> ; Internet; accessed 12 December 2001.

[55] Ibid.

[56] Jonathan Lurie, "Military Justice 50 Years After Nuremberg: Some Reflections on Appearance V. Reality," 28 August 2001, available from <http://www.jagcnet.army.mil/JAGCNETInternet>, Internet; accessed 28 November 2001.

[57] Katharine Seelye, "In A Letter, 300 Law Professors Oppose Tribunals Plan," The New York Times on the Web, 7 December 2001, available from <http://www.nytimes.com/2001/12/08/national>, Internet; accessed 10 December 2001.

[58] Robert A. Levy, "Don't Shred the Constitution to Fight Terror," The Wall Street Journal, 20 November 2001, A18.

[59] Ibid.

[60] Ibid.

[61] Marjorie Cohn, "Let U.N. Try Terrorists," The National Law Journal, 10 December 2001, A21.

[62] Ibid.

[63] "Editorial," USA Today, 30 November, 2001, A11.

[64] Keith B. Richburg and T.R. Reid, "France Cautions U.S. Over Sept. 11 Defendant," The Washington Post, 13 December 2001, A13.

[65] Ibid.

[66] Ibid.

[67] David Scheffer, "Our Credibility is on the Line," Newsweek Web Exclusive, 28 November 2001, available from <http://www.msnbc.com/news/664569.asp>, Internet; accessed 10 December 2001.

[68] Ibid.

[69] Richburg and Reid, A13.

[70] Vernon Loeb, "Allies Called Essential as Terror Hunt Widens," The Washington Post, 22 February 2002, A18.

[71] T.R. Reid, "Europeans Reluctant to Send Terror Suspects to U.S.," The Washington Post, 29 November 2001, A23.

[72] James Gerstenzang and Josh Meyer, "Bush Defends War Tribunals as Necessary," The Los Angles Times, 30 November 2001, A1.

[73] Elizabeth Olson, "World Briefing," 8 December 2001, available from <http://nytimes.com/2001/12/08/international/08BRIE.html>, Internet; accessed 10 December 2001.

[74] William J. Clinton, <u>A National Security Strategy for a Global Age</u> (Washington, D.C.: The White House, December 2000), 35.

[75] Ibid.

[76] Charles W. Gittins, "Military Commissions – Wrong Response to September 11," <u>The Washington Post</u>, 28 November 2001, A16.

# BIBLIOGRAPHY

Aldykiewicz, Jan E., and Geoffrey S. Corn, "Authority to Court-Martial Non-U.S. Military Personnel for Serious Violations Of International Humanitarian Law Committed During Internal Armed Conflicts." Military Law Review, March 2001, 74-152.

Alter, Jonathan. "Consider History. Or Not." 30 November 2001. Available from <http://stacks.msnbc.com/news/665751.asp>. Internet. Accessed 9 December 2001.

_____. "Keeping Order in the Courts." Newsweek, 10 December 2001, 48-49.

Appleman, John A. Military Tribunals and International Crimes. Boston: The Bobbs-Merrill Publishing Company, Inc., 1954.

Bishop, Joseph W., Jr. Justice Under Fire - A Study of Military Law. New York: Charterhouse, 1974.

Bland, Mark A. "An Analysis of the United Nations International Tribunal to Adjudicate War Crimes Committed in The Former Yugoslavia: Parallels, Problems, Prospects." Global Legal Studies Journal II, Spring 1999, 5.

Brown, Bartram S. "Nationality and Internationality in International Humanitarian Law." Stanford Journal of International Law, 1998, 347.

Bush, George W. Military Order – Detention, Treatment and Trial of Certain Non-Citizens on the War Against Terrorism. Washington, D.C.: The White House, 13 November 2001.

Clinton, William J. A National Security Strategy For A Global Age. Washington, D.C.: The White House, December 2000.

_____. Presidential Decision Directive 62. Washington, D.C.: The White House, May 1998.

Cohen, Adam. "Rough Justice." Time, 10 December 2001, 30-37.

Cohn, Marjorie. "Let U.N. Try Terrorists." The National Law Journal, 10 December 2001, 21.

Cohen, Richard. "Liberties Be Damned." The Washington Post, 27 November 2001, sec. A, 13.

Crona, Spencer J., and Richardson, Niel A. "Justice for War Criminals of Invisible Armies: A New Legal and Military Approach to Terrorism." Oklahoma City University Law Review, 1996.

Deans, Bob. "State of The Union Address: Our War Against Terror Is Only Beginning." The Atlanta Journal – Constitution, 30 January 2002, sec. A1.

Dean, John. "Appropriate Justice for Terrorists: Using Military Tribunals Rather Than Criminal Courts." 28 September 2001. Available from <http://writ.news.findlaw.com/scriptsdean/20010928.html>. Internet. Accessed 30 November 2001.

Drew, Kevin. "Tribunals Break Sharply From Civilian Courts." 7 December 2001. Available from <http://www.cnn.com/2001/LAW/12/06/inv.tribunals.explainter/index.html>. Internet. Accessed 4 January 2002.

"Editorial," USA Today. 30 November 2001, sec. A, 11.

"U.S. Justice Would Be An Injustice – UN Must Try Terrorists." Editorial. 6 January 2002. Available from <http://www.guardian.co.uk/Archive/Article/0,4273,4329988,00.html>. Internet. Accessed 8 February 2002.

Farkas, Michael C. "If It's War, Treat It That Way." Proceedings, United States Naval Institute, December 2001.

Friedman, Leon. Law of War: A Documentary History, Vols. I & II. New York: Random House, 1972.

Gagner, Phillip A. "The Bush Administration's Claim That Even Citizens Can Be Brought Before Military Tribunals, And Why It Should Never Be Put Into Place." 26 December 2001. Available from <http://writ.findlaw.com/commentary/20011226/gagner.html>. Internet. Accessed 18 February 2002.

Gearan, Anne. "ABA Panel Supports Limited Military Trials." The Washington Post, 8 January 2002, sec. A, 2.

Geneva Convention for the Armed Forces in the Field. 12 August 1949.

Gerstenzang, James and Josh Meyer. "Bush Defends War Tribunals as Necessary." The Los Angles Times, 30 November 2001, sec. A, 1.

Gittins, Charles W. "Military Commissions – Wrong Response to September 11." The Washington Post, 28 November 2001, sec. A, 16.

Glaberson, William. "Tribunal Comparison Taints Courts-Martial, Military Lawyers Say." 2 December 2001. Available from <http://nytimes.com>. Internet. Accessed 12 December 2001.

Glueck, Sheldon. War Criminals – Their Prosecution & Punishment. New York: Alfred A. Knopf, 1944.

Gold, Phillip "Military Courts Are American Way – Military Justice Can Deal with Enemies More Efficiently." The Washington Times, 12 December 2001, sec A, 21.

Gonzales, Alberto R. "Martial Justice, Full and Fair." New York Times, 30 November 2001.

Grigorian, Ellen. The International Criminal Court Treaty: Description, Policy Issues, and Congressional Concerns. Washington, D.C.: Congressional Research Service, Library of Congress, 6 January 1999.

Grossman, Joel B. "Careless with The Constitution? The Problem with Military Tribunals." 29 November 2001. Available from <http://writ.news.findlaw.com/commentary/20011129_grossman.html>. Internet. Accessed 11 February 2001.

Karon, Tony. "Why Trials Matter in the war Against Terrorism." Available from <http://www.time.com/time/world>. Internet. Accessed 10 January 2002.

Kaufman, Stephen. "Establishment of Military Tribunals Is Debated in the U.S." U.S. Department of State, International Information Programs, 28 November. Available from <http://usinfo.state.gov/topical/rights/law.htm>. Internet. Accessed 22 December 2001.

Lardner, George Jr. "Democrats Blast Order on Tribunals." The Washington Post, 29 November 2001, sec. A, 22.

Lehrer, Jim. "Terror Tribunals." Jim Lehrer's NewsHour Transcript, 14 November 2001. Available from <http://www.pbs.org/newshour/bb/law/july-dec01/tribunal_11-14.html>. Internet. Accessed 29 November 2001.

_____. "Who Is A War Criminal?" Jim Lehrer's NewsHour Transcript, 30 August 2001. Available from <http://www.pbs.org/newshour/bb/europe/yugoslavia/july-dec01/criminal_8-30.html>. Internet. Accessed 29 November 2001.

Levy, Robert A. "Don't Shred the Constitution to Fight Terror." The Wall Street Journal, 20 November 2001, sec. A, 18.

Loeb, Vernon. "Allies Called Essential as Terror Hunt Widens." The Washington Post. 22 February 2002, sec. A, 18.

Lurie, Jonathan. "Military Justice 50 Years After Nuremberg: Some Reflections On Appearance V. Reality." 28 August 2001. Available from <http://www.jagcnet.army.mil/JAGCNETInternet>. Internet. Accessed 28 November 2001.

The National Institute of Military Justice. "Crimes of War Project." 30 February 2002. Available from <http://www.nimj.com/Home.asp>. Internet. Accessed 12 March 2002.

O'Hara-Foster, Brigid, and Lauren Comiteau. "Justice Goes Global." Time Canada, 27 July 1998, 32.

Olson, Elizabeth. "World Briefing." 8 December 2001. Available from <http://nytimes.com/2001/12/08/international/08BRIE.html>. Internet. Accessed 10 December 2001.

Maga, Tim. Judgment at Tokyo – The Japanese War Crimes Trials. Lexington: The University Press of Kentucky, 2001.

Mayers, Lewis. The American Legal System. New York: Harper & Brothers Publishers, 1955.

Moore, John N. National Security Law. Durham: Durham Carolina Academic Press, 1990.

Murray, Frank J. "U.S. Says Tribunals Just for Terror Leaders." The Washington Times, 12 December 2001, sec A, 1.

Neave, Airey. On Trial at Nuremberg. Boston: Little, Brown and Company Publishing Co. 1978.

Newton, Michael A. "Continuum Crimes: Military Jurisdiction over Foreign Nationals Who Commit International Crimes." Military Law Review, 1996, 20.

Orenstein, James. "Rooting Out Terrorist Just Became Harder." 6 December 2001. Available from <http://www.nytimes.com/2001/12/06/opinion/06OREN.html>. Internet. Accessed 12 December 2001.

"Proclamation Number 2561, 2 July 1942," Federal Register 5101 (1964).

Purdy, Matthew. "Bush's New Rules to Fight Terror Transform the Legal Landscape." The New York Times, 25 November 2001, sec A, 1.

Reid, T.R. "Europeans Reluctant to Send Terror Suspects to U.S." The Washington Post, 29 November 2001, sec A, 23.

Richburg, Keith B., and T.R. Reid. "France Cautions U.S. Over Sept. 11 Defendant." The Washington Post, 13 December 2001, sec. A, 13.

Richter, Paul. "U.S. Lays Plans For Interrogation, Trials." The Los Angles Times, 12 December 2001, sec A, 1.

Scharf, Michael P. "Defining Terrorism as the Peace Time Equivalent of War Crimes: A Case of Too Much Convergence Between International Humanitarian Law and International Criminal Law." ILSAJ International Law, 2001.

Scheffer, David. "Our Credibility Is on the Line." 28 November 2001. Available from <http://www.msnbc.com/news/664569.asp>. Internet. Accessed 10 December 2001.

Schwarzenberger, George. International Law as Applied by International Courts and Tribunals, Vol. II, Law of Armed Conflict. New York: Stevenson & Sons, 1968.

Seelye, Katharine. "In a Letter, 300 Law Professors Oppose Tribunals Plan." 7 December 2001. Available from <http://www.nytimes.com/2001/12/08/national>. Internet. Accessed 10 December 2001.

Skiba, Katherine M. "Quick Action Against bin Laden Called Difficult." Milwaukee Journal Sentinel, 26 September 2001, sec. A, 6.

Solis, Gary D. "Are We Really a War?" Proceedings, United States Naval Institute, December 2001.

Supreme Court Case, Ex Parte Quirin, 317 U.S. 1, 45 (1942).

Taylor, Stuart, Jr. "Before the Bar of History." 10 December 2001. Available from <http://stacks.msnbc.com/news/666229.asp>. Internet. Accessed 12 December 2001.

The ABA Terrorism Task Force Report on Military Tribunals. "A Realistic Step in the Right Direction." Available from <http://www.abanet.org>. Internet. Accessed 8 February 2001.

Toner, Robin. "Despite Some Concerns, Civil Liberties Are Taking a Back Seat." 18 November 2001. Available from <http://www.nytimes.com/2001/11/18/politics/18LIBE.html>. Internet. Accessed 18 November 2001.

Tyrangiel, Josh. "And Justice For...." Time, 26 November 2001, 66-67.

The United States Constitution. Article II.

U.S. Department of the Army. Law of Land Warfare. Army Field Manual 27-10. Washington, D.C.: U.S. Department of the Army, July 1956.

United States Supreme Court. In re Yamashita, 327 U.S. 1, (1946).

Walzer, Michael. "First, Define the Battlefield." New York Times, 21 September 2001, sec A, 35.

The War Crimes Act of 1996. U.S. Code. 18 U.S.C. 2441 (1996).

Wedgewood, Ruth. "Responding to Terrorism: The Strikes Against bin Laden." Yale International Law Journal, 1999.

Wickham, De Wayne. "Even Terrorist Have Civil Rights." USA Today, 27 November 2001, sec A, 15.

Wiener, Frederick W. Civilians Under Military Justice. Chicago: The University of Chicago Press, 1967.